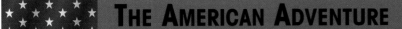

THE GREAT LAND RUSH

SALLY SENZELL ISAACS

Heinemann Library
Chicago, Illinois

© 2004 Heinemann Library
a division of Reed Elsevier Inc.
Chicago, Illinois

Customer Service 888-454-2279

Visit our website at www.heinemannlibrary.com

Produced for Heinemann Library by
   Bender Richardson White.
Editor: Lionel Bender
Designer and Page Makeup: Ben White
Picture Researcher: Cathy Stastny
Production Controller: Kim Richardson

07 06 05 04 03
10 9 8 7 6 5 4 3 2 1

Printed and bound by Lake Book Manufacturing, Inc.

Library of Congress Cataloging-in-Publication Data.
Isaacs, Sally Senzell, 1950-
    The great land rush / Sally Senzell Isaacs.
       p. cm.--(The American adventure)
    Includes bibliographical references (p.) and index.
    Contents: Indian territory--Settlers on the plains--The Indian
    wars--More land needed--Getting ready to rush--The first
    great land rush--The new town of Guthrie--Building a new
    life--Plowing the land--Changing the American Indians.
       ISBN 1-4034-2505-1 – ISBN 1-4034-4771-3 (pbk.)
    1. Oklahoma–History--Land Rush, 1889--Juvenile literature.
    2. Oklahoma–History--Land Rush, 1893--Juvenile literature.
    3. Indian Territory--History--Juvenile literature. 4. Indians of
    North America--Land tenure--Oklahoma--History--19th
    century--Juvenile literature. 5. Frontier and pioneer life--
    Oklahoma--Juvenile literature. 6. Great Plains--History--19th
    century--Juvenile literature. 7. Indians of North America--Land
    tenure--Great Plains--History--19th century--Juvenile literature.
    8. Frontier and pioneer life--Great Plains--Juvenile literature.
    [1. Oklahoma--History--Land Rush, 1893. 2. Indians of North
    America--Land tenure. 3. Frontier and pioneer life--Oklahoma.
    4. Great Plains--History--19th century. 5. Frontier and pioneer
    life--Great Plains.]
    I. Title.
    F699.I83 2003
    976.6'04--dc21

                                      2003005586

Special thanks to Mike Carpenter and Geof Knight at Heinemann
Library for editorial and design guidance and direction.

Acknowledgments
The producers and publishers are grateful to the following for
permission to reproduce copyright material:
Corbis Images, pages 10, 23. Corbis Images/Bettmann, page
13. Peter Newark's American Pictures, pages 6, 9, 14, 16, 19,
20, 25. Library of Congress, Washington D.C., U.S.A., page 26.

Illustrations by John James
Maps by Stefan Chabluk
Cover art by John James

QUOTATIONS

Major quotations used in this book come from the
following sources. Some of the quotations have been
abridged for clarity.

Page 10: Crazy Horse quote from *History of US:
Reconstruction and Reform* by Joy Hakim. Oxford and
New York: Oxford University Press, 1994, page 85.

Pages 15 and 16: Hank Henry quotes from
http://www.mailtribune.com/prime/archive. Copyright
2000 *The Mail Tribune*, Medford, Oregon.

Page 16: William Howard quote originally from *Harper's
Weekly 33* (May 18, 1889): 391-94. Reprinted in
Eyewitness to the American West edited by David
Colbert. New York: Viking Penguin, 1998, page 198.

Page 20: Arapahoe Arrow quote from *Arapahoe Arrow*
April 29, 1892. Vol. 1#1. Will C. Seaman and Frank
Fillmore, Publishers. Found at website:
http://freepages.genealogy.rootsweb.com/
   ~swokla/custer/Arrow.html

Page 24: Lone Wolf quote and quote about education
from *The West* by Geoffrey C. Ward. Boston: Little,
Brown and Company, 1996, pages 360-361.

The Author
Sally Senzell Isaacs is a professional writer and
editor of nonfiction books for children. She
graduated from Indiana University, earning a B.S.
degree in Education with majors in American
History and Sociology. She is the author of the nine
titles in the *America in the Time of...* series
published by Heinemann Library and of the first
sixteen titles in Heinemann Library's *Picture the
Past* series. Sally Senzell Isaacs lives in New
Jersey with her husband and two children.

The Consultant
Our thanks to William D. Welge, CA, director
Research Division, Oklahoma Historical Society, for
his comments in the preparation of this book.

Note to the Reader
Some words are shown in bold, like **this**.
You can find out what they mean by looking in the
glossary on page 30.

ABOUT THIS BOOK

This book is about the Oklahoma land rush of 1889 to 1895 and other events in America surrounding it. The term *America* means the United States of America (also called the U.S.)

On five separate occasions during these years, the United States government gave away land very cheaply to anyone willing to build on it. It led to great rushes—or "runs"—to claim land in the West. The land was in Indian Territory (present-day Oklahoma). In the late 1820s and throughout the 1830s , the U.S. government promised this land to American Indians in order to get them to leave their land east of the Mississippi River. This book tries to show the two different viewpoints of the great land rush: the **settlers'** view and the American Indians' view.

CONTENTS

ABOUT THE SERIES

The American Adventure is a series of books about important events that shaped the United States of America. Each book focuses on one event. While learning about the event, the reader will also learn how the people and places of the time period influenced the nation's future. The little illustrations at the top left of each two-page article are a symbol of the times. They are identified in the Contents on page 3.

▼ This map shows the United States today, with the **borders** and names of all the states. Refer to this map, or to the one on pages 28 and 29, to locate places talked about in this book.

AMERICA'S STORY

Throughout the book, the yellow panels showing a new town building contain information that tells the more general history of the United States of America.

THE FEATURE STORY

The green panels, showing a settler's horsedrawn wagon, contain more detailed information about the Oklahoma land rush, this book's feature event.

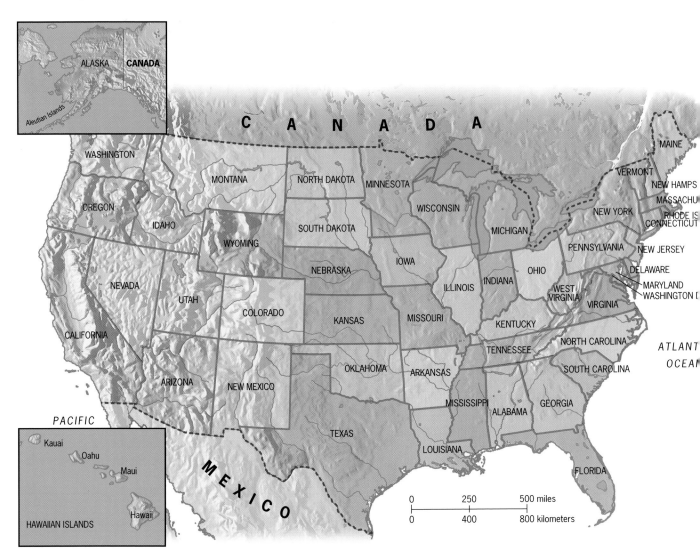

THE GREAT LAND RUSH
INTRODUCTION

When Christopher Columbus's ships reached the Americas in 1492, between about 15 and 20 million American Indians lived on the continent. For thousands of years, their ancestors had lived in scattered villages or in groups of roaming hunters.

Columbus and other explorers—mainly from Spain, France, and England—thought they had found a New World. The thick forests and sparkling rivers promised a place that could make people rich. There might even be gold! Some explorers found the American Indians helpful. The Indians guided explorers, and later **settlers,** over the unknown land. The Indians also provided food and horses to the newcomers. But some explorers were cruel to the Indians. The explorers captured Indians and made them slaves.

Over the next 200 years, millions of **immigrants** from Europe moved to North America. They built houses, farms, and towns. At first these new settlers stayed on the coast of the Atlantic Ocean. As areas became crowded, people moved westward. Was the continent large enough for millions of newcomers to live with the millions of American Indians? History tells us there was not.

First, there was the problem of disease. Hundreds of thousands of American Indians died from diseases that the settlers carried. Then there was the problem of land. Most white Americans were filled with a spirit of growth and optimism. Many believed in Manifest Destiny, which meant that the nation of cities, towns, farms, ranches—and railroads to connect them—should stretch from ocean to ocean. In the end, the settlers used the power of the United States lawmakers and the United States Army to take over the American Indians' homeland. The Oklahoma land rush was part of this process.

INDIAN TERRITORY

Long ago, North America was dotted with thousands of American Indian villages. These people belonged to hundreds of separate tribes who spoke different languages and had different beliefs. Eventually they would all share a common problem: they would be forced to leave their homeland.

Millions of people came to America from other countries with the hope of owning land and building a future. By the 1800s, most **settlers** felt they had a right to live on American Indian land. Some settlers believed that the American Indians could stay on their land if they learned the ways of the settlers. Many tribes did not want to change their **customs.** Others, now called the **Five Civilized Tribes,** already were successful farmers. The Cherokee, Chickasaw, Choctaw, Creek, and Seminole tribes developed methods of planting crops and raising cattle. They had laws, schools, and churches. These five tribes lived in the Carolinas, Georgia, Alabama, Mississippi, Tennessee, and Florida.

By 1828, many white people saw all American Indians as a barrier to the growth of the nation. About that time, the United States government chose land in present-day Oklahoma and called it Indian **Territory.** The government tried to make deals, called **treaties,** with Indian tribes. The government promised land, food, and clothing in Indian Territory if the Five Civilized Tribes would give up their land.

Indian Removal Act
Some Indians moved peacefully, but others would not. In 1830, the U.S. **Congress** passed the Indian Removal Act. It stated that all American Indians must move west of the Mississippi River. Members of the Five Civilized Tribes were forced to Indian Territory, where they joined tribes already living there. They included the Wichita, Quapaw, and Osage.

INDIAN TERRITORY
Through much of the 1800s, present-day Oklahoma was called Indian Territory. The land seemed too dry and useless for settlers to desire it. Around 1830, the U.S. government began giving land to the Five Civilized Tribes. President Andrew Jackson promised that each tribe could be an independent nation and keep the land "as long as grass grows and water runs."

In 1867, the U.S. government also moved the Kiowa, Comanche, and Arapaho from Kansas and Nebraska to Indian Territory.

▼ The Arapaho tribes had once lived on the **Great Plains.** They hunted buffalo, which provided most of their food. This photo shows Arapahos in Indian Territory with officials from the government. Now they were expected to be farmers, not hunters.

6

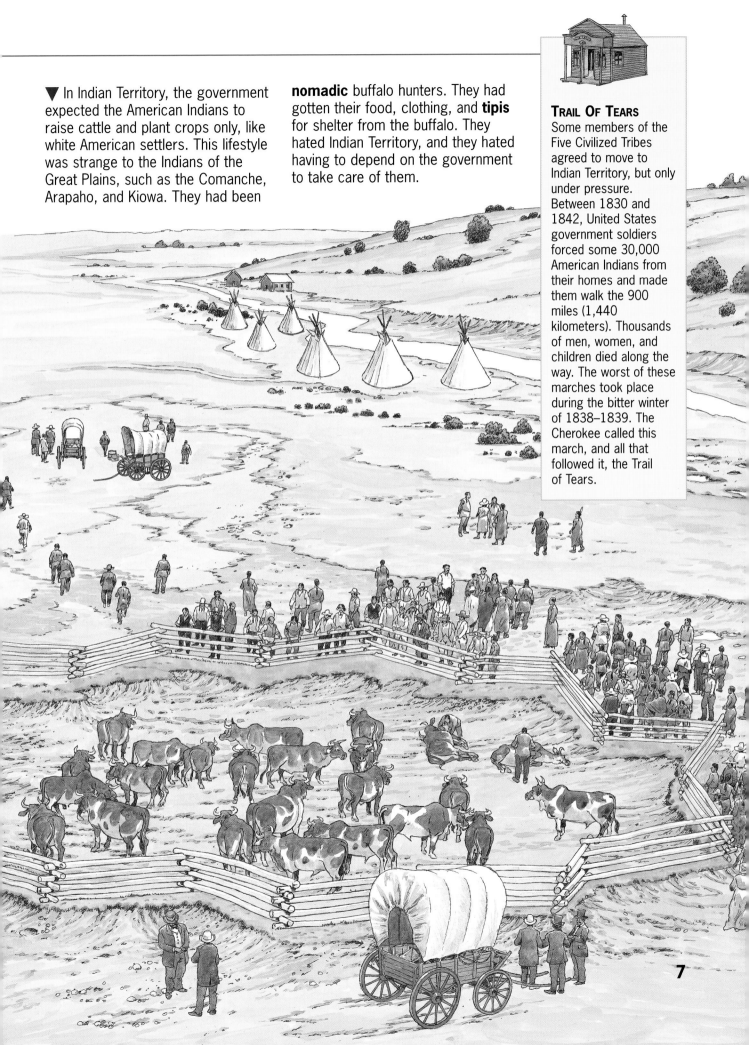

In Indian Territory, the government expected the American Indians to raise cattle and plant crops only, like white American settlers. This lifestyle was strange to the Indians of the Great Plains, such as the Comanche, Arapaho, and Kiowa. They had been nomadic buffalo hunters. They had gotten their food, clothing, and **tipis** for shelter from the buffalo. They hated Indian Territory, and they hated having to depend on the government to take care of them.

TRAIL OF TEARS

Some members of the Five Civilized Tribes agreed to move to Indian Territory, but only under pressure. Between 1830 and 1842, United States government soldiers forced some 30,000 American Indians from their homes and made them walk the 900 miles (1,440 kilometers). Thousands of men, women, and children died along the way. The worst of these marches took place during the bitter winter of 1838–1839. The Cherokee called this march, and all that followed it, the Trail of Tears.

SETTLERS ON THE PLAINS

Indian Territory was just a small part of a big area of treeless land called the Great Plains. Two different kinds of people wanted to live on the Great Plains: American Indians and settlers. Could they share this land?

The Plains Indians had lived on this land for thousands of years. Some lived on farms, but most moved their villages frequently as they followed buffalo herds. They did not own the land. They believed that land, like air and water, belonged to everyone.

By the 1830s, however, thousands of other people were hungry to own land. They came from towns and farms in the East as well as from other countries. They heard about the wide-open **Great Plains** and wanted to own a **homestead,** which included a house and land. Most of these people thought the Indians had no right to stop them. In 1862, the United States government agreed with these people. **Congress** passed the Homestead Act. It gave 160 acres (65 hectares—about the size of 70 soccer fields) to any **settler** who paid a small fee and agreed to work the land for five years. The act provided homes for 400,000 to 600,000 settlers.

A hard life

The homesteaders faced a difficult life. Because the land had few trees, they had to build sod homes out of blocks of earth, grass, and roots. Little air or sunlight came into the house. But if it rained, water dripped through the roof to turn the dirt floor into mud. The weather brought problems to the new farms: hot, dry summers, and freezing blizzards and ice storms. Insects invaded, too. At least a third of the newcomers turned around and went home. Most stayed and solved their problems as best they could. Luckily there were some rainy summers. Many farmers found ways to grow wheat and to bring water to their crops by digging ditches from rivers to their fields.

AMERICA'S 100TH BIRTHDAY
In 1876, millions of U.S. citizens went to the centennial celebration in Philadelphia. They saw these new inventions: the washing machine, the sewing machine, and the typewriter. Two months earlier, Alexander Graham Bell had displayed his new telephone. The next year, 1877, Thomas Edison invented the phonograph. Two years later, he invented the electric light bulb.

▶ A swarm of **locusts** is driving this family mad! In the 1870s, the insects were a terrible problem. They ate the corn and wheat in the fields and the vegetables in the gardens. Many farmers lost all their money because locusts destroyed their farms. Farmers often borrowed money from a bank to buy seeds and farm machines. When their crops were destroyed, they could not pay back the bank. The bank owned the farm, and the family was forced to move out.

▲ This family lived in a sod house in Nebraska. Before 1865, millions of African Americans were **slaves** who were made to work on large farms in the South. The U.S. government outlawed slavery, but many Southern landowners would not pay former slaves much to continue to work for them.
Thousands of African Americans decided to become homesteaders on the Great Plains. This photograph was taken in 1887.

BUFFALO
Railroad companies were quickly laying tracks across the Great Plains. Trains brought more settlers. In just a few years, non-American Indian hunters had killed four million buffalo. Some sold the buffalo meat to feed the railroad workers. Others shot buffalo from train windows just for fun. With the buffalo gone, the Plains Indians could not survive.

9

THE INDIAN WARS

As settlers, ranchers, and railroad companies moved to the Great Plains, the United States government did everything possible to make the Plains Indians leave. Some tribes left for a promise of a peaceful life. Others were forced out by the guns of the United States Army.

The government set up **reservations—** land where Indians would live away from the **settlers.** Many of these reservations were in present-day North Dakota, South Dakota, and Wyoming. Government officials set up offices on the reservations and promised to help the tribes start a new life by giving them food, guns, and blankets. But the government broke most of its promises. The size of the reservations kept shrinking. The money spent on the Indians shrank, too.

Instead of hunting, the Indians stood in line to wait for food and clothing. Chief Crazy Horse, a Sioux leader, said, "We preferred hunting to a life of **idleness** on the reservation where we were driven against our will. At times we did not get enough to eat, and we were not allowed to leave the reservation to hunt.… All we wanted was peace and to be left alone."

The government sent soldiers to the Great Plains to try keep things peaceful. This was a nearly impossible job. The soldiers tried to keep settlers off the reservations and keep American Indians on the reservations.

▼ The Chirichua Apaches fought many battles against United States soldiers in Arizona and New Mexico. In 1886, their leader, Geronimo, (front row, third from right) and others were taken by train to a prison in Texas. Eventually Geronimo was allowed to settle in Oklahoma.

10

A bitter end

By 1870, the Sioux, Cheyenne, and Arapaho people were living in the Black Hills of South Dakota. In 1874, the government wanted to buy this land to mine gold that had just been found there. They wanted the American Indians to move to a reservation 250 miles (402 kilometers) away. For the next two years, the Sioux leader, Sitting Bull, refused to give up the land. What followed was one of many brutal battles between American Indians and soldiers. In the end, the Indians could not run away from the United States government. By 1890, thousands of Plains Indians had starved to death or were killed in battle. The rest lived on reservations.

▼ Many western tribes performed a Ghost Dance to give themselves hope for their future. They believed that the dance would take away all bad things from their past. Murdered relatives, dead buffalo, and lost land would return. White soldiers were afraid of this ceremony.

LOST INDIAN LAND
1876 Sioux, Cheyenne, and Arapaho defeat Lieutenant Colonel George Custer at Little Bighorn River in present-day Montana.
1877 The Nez Perce fight to protect their land in Washington and Idaho, but in 1877 Chief Joseph **surrenders.** The army takes what is left of his people to a disease-filled part of Indian Territory.
1886 Apache chief Geronimo surrenders and moves his people to a reservation.
1890 The last battle between Indians and the army is fought at Wounded Knee Creek, South Dakota. Hundreds of Indians are killed.

11

MORE LAND NEEDED

By 1870, the United States was becoming a big nation. There were 38 states. Factories in the East provided jobs for many people and made things that Americans could afford to buy. Railroad tracks crossed the entire continent, making a coast-to-coast trip possible in just ten days.

Millions of **immigrants** came to the United States to follow their dreams for freedom, jobs, and land. Thousands of people headed west when they heard that gold and silver had been discovered in California and Nevada. Thousands more lived on **homesteads** in the **Great Plains.** They grew wheat so successfully that it was sold and shipped all over America. The Great Plains was called "the nation's bread basket." As the country grew, U.S. citizens wanted more land. Indian **Territory,** which once seemed useless, began to look attractive. Of course it had been promised to the American Indians forever, but that promise would not stand in the way.

Dividing up Indian Territory

The U.S. government had divided Indian Territory among many tribes. There was a section in the middle of the territory that was not assigned, or given in writing, to a tribe. Beginning in 1879, settlers who called themselves **boomers** tried to move onto this land. United States soldiers kept throwing them out. It would be ten more years before **Congress** made this **Unassigned Land** available to homesteaders.

The Dawes Act

In 1887, Congress passed the Dawes Act (an act is a rule, law or decision of government). It took away a tribe's right to own vast open spaces. Instead it gave each Indian family 160 acres (65 hectares) of land. A single person got 40 or 80 acres (16 or 32 hectares). After the American Indians received their portions, the rest of the land could be sold to white settlers. The government said that the act would help the Indians to become farmers. But many Indians were not interested in farming. They sold their land to settlers, often in unfair dealings. In all, American Indians lost 90 million acres of land.

DAVID PAYNE
David Payne was a colorful leader of the boomers. At least twice a year for four years, he led hundreds of covered wagons across the Indian Territory border. Each time, soldiers made them turn back. Payne was arrested more than once, but this did not stop him. He died of illness in 1884 without becoming an Oklahoma citizen.

CATTLE DRIVES
In the 1870s, people in the East wanted beef on their tables. Cowboys led thousands of cattle from Texas through Indian Territory on their way to train stops in Kansas. Some tribes charged high prices to let the cattle drives pass through their land.

▶ From 1880 to 1885, boomers gathered at the Kansas-Oklahoma border. Many rode in wagons with signs that said "Oklahoma or Bust." Time after time, they tried to cross the border to move into Indian Territory. Each time, United States soldiers made them turn around and leave.

12

◀ This is Fort Washakie, a **reservation** started for the Shoshone tribe in Wyoming in the 1800s. The people are performing a tribal dance. The fort was named after a Shoshone chief who served in the United States Army.

GETTING READY TO RUSH

The boomers kept trying to sneak into the Unassigned Land. They also kept going to Washington to convince the president and Congress to open the Unassigned Land to homesteaders. Finally they got what they wanted.

On March 2, 1889, President Benjamin Harrison signed a new law. It declared that the Unassigned Land would be opened for homesteaders. This area was about 30 miles (48 kilometers) wide and 50 miles (80 kilometers) long.

All kinds of people celebrated the opening of this land. There were the thousands of people who wanted to move to the land. Some were factory workers from eastern towns who had lost their jobs. Others were farmers in the Midwest who had lost their crops to bad weather.

Cattle drives and railroads
Cattle owners were happy to have the land divided up among individuals. It would be easier for them to buy or rent grazing land for their animals along the cattle drives from Texas to Kansas. Railroad companies also celebrated. Their trains could bring passengers and goods to the new **homesteads** in Oklahoma. The Santa Fe Railroad already had a station built in the middle of the Unassigned Land.

Government workers divided up the land like a checkerboard. Stones marked off the 160-acre (65-hectare) sections. On April 22, 1889, at 12:00 noon—not a second before—people would be allowed to race out to Oklahoma and **claim** a section.

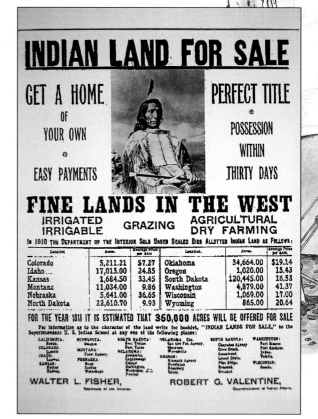

▲ A 1911 poster advertising Indian land for sale. There were many advertisements like this in land rush days. Little by little, American Indians lost their hunting grounds and any means of taking care of themselves in their traditional ways. Their population dropped greatly. They sold their land to the U.S. government and moved to **reservations.**

SOONERS
The night before the race, some cheaters sneaked past the guards and staked their claims. Most of these cheaters were caught. They were nicknamed **sooners** because they had made their claims too soon. The Sooner State is still the nickname of Oklahoma.

14

▼ Thousands of people came from far and near to claim a piece of land in Indian **Territory.** For a few days before April 22, these people lived in tents with their belongings in wagons. They waited for noon, when a signal would start the race, and they could ride their horses out to stake their claims. Others would ride bicycles or simply run.

Rules of the race

Three days before the race, hopeful homesteaders were allowed to enter Cherokee Outlet in the north and Chickasaw country in the south. The land was available to men and women who were over the age of 21. They had to be United States citizens or declare that they planned to become citizens. At the sound of a bugle, cannon, or pistol firing, a person ran to a section of land and hammered in a pole with his or her name on it. Then he or she went to the **land office** to make the claim and pay a $15 fee. (Today that is worth about $280.)

A BOOMER'S STORY
Hank Henry's father bumped along in a wagon when his family claimed a piece of land that day. In an article in the Medford, Oregon, *Mail Tribune*, Mr. Henry described his father's memory: "The United States Army was called up to oversee the race for these unclaimed lands. A starting line stretched for several miles. Waiting eagerly were men on horseback ready to race to a certain piece of land the family had picked out during an earlier inspection tour."

THE FIRST GREAT LAND RUSH

"My dad remembered that it was a warm April day in 1889 as hundreds milled around or went visiting other wagons while waiting for the race to start … The dust was awful, and it got even worse when the horses were frightened by several cannons fired to signal the opening of the race."

Those were the words of Hank Henry as he described his father's time at the land rush. He continued, " … the wagons bounced over hills and gullies with such abandon that it was all the passengers could do to hang on. On Dad's wagon, everybody got down on the floor and stayed there."

When the bugle blasted, cannons were fired, and everyone took off. William Howard saw the event. He wrote in *Harper's Weekly* magazine on May 18, 1889, about a runner he saw. "One man left the line with the others, carrying on his back a tent, a blanket, some camp dishes, an axe, and provisions for two days. He ran down the railway track for six miles, and reached his **claim** in just sixty minutes. He fell down under a tree, unable to speak or see."

▼ Another land rush took place on September 16, 1893, on land called the Cherokee Outlet. At the start of the race, horseback riders jumped into the lead in front of the wagons and runners. More than 100,000 people raced to claim 42,000 sections of land.

CHILDREN
The land rush was a fun-filled adventure for some children. As grown-ups stood in line at the **land office,** children ran to a creek and filled a bucket with water. They sold water to the grown-ups for five cents a cup. (Today that is worth almost a dollar.)

▶ This father and uncle rode horses to quickly claim a piece of land and set up a tent. The rest of the family followed in a wagon filled with their belongings. The family probably soon replaced the tent with a stronger building. Some people had to give up their claims because they were in the middle of a street.

RUSHING BY TRAIN
Mr. Howard wrote about people arriving by train at 1:20 P.M. Much of the land was already "dotted white with tents and sprinkled thick with men running about in all directions…. Men jumped from the roofs of the moving cars. … Many … squeeze(d) through the windows in order to get a fair start at the head of the crowd."

New towns

Within a few hours, all 3,000 square miles (7,770 square kilometers) were filled with people. Several towns were born that day. By sundown, Guthrie had gone from a population of 0 to 15,000. Oklahoma City had 10,000 people. For the first few days, people lived in their tents or wagons and fought over their claims. Food and water could be bought, but only at a high price. Settlers had little money so they often went hungry and thirsty.

THE NEW TOWN OF GUTHRIE

When the United States government first decided to open the land to settlers, it made no plans to organize the land into towns. But the settlers of Guthrie did that themselves. In less than a week, they had chosen a mayor and laid out the town's streets.

▼ The new citizens of Guthrie built their town quickly. On this street, people are turning their tents into stores and offices. Supply wagons bring supplies, groceries, and furniture from the East.

As the dust settled from the first land rush, the new citizens of Guthrie started building a town. Three men set up a bank using a pot-bellied stove as a safe until they could afford a real one. A man who really was a blacksmith decided that the town needed a dentist. He hung a sign outside his tent declaring that he could fix teeth. Carpenters started putting together buildings, and writers started printing newspapers. An elderly woman, calling herself Button Mary, started a business sewing buttons onto shirts for a dime each. In a few months, Guthrie had six banks, sixteen barbers, fifteen hotels, and nine churches.

Oklahoma Territory

In May, 1890, **Congress** passed the Oklahoma Organic Act. It turned most of the western part of Indian Territory into Oklahoma Territory. Any new towns would belong to this new territory. Like the states, Oklahoma had a governor, a supreme court, and elected lawmakers. Guthrie, the largest town at the time, became the capital.

From 1891 to 1895, the U.S. government bought more American Indian land and opened it for homesteaders. In those years, there were four more land rushes.

▼ The first city directory in Guthrie (August 1889) showed 6 banks, 16 barbers, 16 blacksmiths or wagon makers, 17 carpenters and builders, 2 cigar manufacturers, 7 hardware stores, 15 hotels, 19 pharmacists, 22 lumber dealers, 5 photographers, 39 doctors, 40 restaurants, 9 churches, 5 newspapers, a telegraph office, an electric plant, and 81 lawyers (mostly for filing claims).

Holding Down A Lot In Guthrie 26

▲ Shortly after April 22, this family sits on the land they **claimed** to keep others away from it.

LAND RUSHES
In all, there were five land rushes, or land runs, in Oklahoma.
April 22, 1889
Unassigned Land.
The towns of Guthrie, Oklahoma City, Kingfisher, El Reno, Norman, and Stillwater all grew out of this land rush.
September 22, 1891
Sac-Fox, Iowa, Shawnee, and Potawatomi Indian **reservations**
April 19, 1892
Cheyenne and Arapaho reservations
September 16, 1893
Cherokee Outlet, and Tonkawa and Pawnee reservations
May 25, 1895
Mexican Kickapoo reservation.

CHEROKEE OUTLET
While many members of other American Indian nations accepted the 160-acre (65-hectare) land sections, the Cherokee Nation did not. But by 1893, the Cherokees were running out of money, and they decided to sell part of their land, called the Cherokee Outlet, to the U.S. government for $1.40 per acre. (That is worth $27.50 today.)
In September 1893, the largest land rush ever was held in the Cherokee Outlet. The area was larger than the state of Massachusetts.

BUILDING A NEW LIFE

In the new town of Arapahoe, a newspaper article on April 29, 1892, reported: "Settlers are on their claims and many of them are making gardens and putting in crops. So come to Arapahoe .... We feel perfectly safe in predicting that Arapahoe .... will be one of the most healthy cities in the territory."

BOLEY, OK
There were 26 towns in Oklahoma set up by African Americans. Boley was one of them. White leaders in other towns refused to talk to Boley's leaders. White people passed a law to keep black people from voting in state elections. In the early 1900s, Boley had 4,000 people. There were schools from elementary level through junior college.

At first the **homesteaders** celebrated their new **claims.** Then they faced the truth. Much of the soil looked like red dust. Water was scarce. Many settlers had just a few dollars to feed their families until they could grow crops. Some sold their claims after a few months because they were afraid their families would starve. Others, with more money, worked hard and prayed for rain.

▼ This poster from 1895 is selling "choice farming land" in Kansas. The land is owned by the Union Pacific Railroad Company.

Trains and wagons brought supplies from eastern cities. With little money, many families ate inexpensive foods, such as soup and bread. Some people earned a living by cooking food for others. One store in Arapahoe advertised "a good square meal consisting of ham and eggs, hot biscuits and butter, good coffee, fruit pie, etc. Only 25 cents. Coffee and doughnuts 10 cents."

Mixes of people and cultures
Not everybody was a farmer. Ads in a 1892 *Arapahoe Arrow* show ads for a sign painter, lawyer, druggist, baker, and candle maker. Every town also hired at least one teacher. Schools usually were one-room cabins where children of all ages learned together.

The settlers spent the first several months getting to know one another. They came from all 38 states and from other countries, too. African Americans, Mexicans, American Indians, and whites now all shared land that was once called Indian **Territory.** It was now known as Oklahoma Territory.

20

▼ This is a cutaway of a general store in one of the new towns in Oklahoma Territory. Unlike settlers in the early 1800s, in the late 1800s people no longer made everything they needed. They went to stores to buy clothes, furniture, tools, and even bread.

LAND FOR SALE
Some people tried to sell their land to make money. The railroad sometimes paid fair money for land. But one man sold all his land, a $12 tent, $6 worth of blankets, and some food for $4.

PLOWING THE LAND

Many homesteaders turned their land into a farming business. They borrowed money to buy fences, seeds, and machines for planting and harvesting their crops. Some years were very successful. Others were disasters. Success depended on the weather.

Earlier in American history, almost everyone was a farmer. Most people grew the food they needed for their families. They made their own furniture and their clothes, too. By 1890, fewer people were farmers. Some people were furniture makers and others were tailors. People sold their goods through stores. Farmers grew more food than they needed. Farmers from the **Great Plains** sold and shipped wheat, corn, barley, and oat products around the world. Others raised cattle and provided much of the nation's beef.

Farmers depended on good weather. For many years of the 1880s, the fields were drenched with rain. Farmers celebrated. Some even believed the saying, "Rain follows the plow." They believed that if people moved to an area and started shaking up the ground with trains, wagons, and plows, they could make rain. Of course, they were wrong.

Dry years
Luck ran out for the farmers in the 1890s. Year after year, there was little rain, and people gave little thought to using the land wisely. Trees had been cut down. Prairie grass had been plowed under. Nothing was left to keep the soil in place when a strong wind blew. The soil dried up and the crops died. In earlier years, farmers would leave worn-out fields and move west. But now there was no unused land to move to.

FARM MACHINES
In the 1830s, Cyrus McCormick developed his famous reaper. It was a machine, pulled by horses or mules, that quickly cut wheat in a large field. McCormick made the machines in a factory in Chicago and sent them to farms by train. In 1879, the factory made 18,790 reapers. In 1881, it made 49,000.

22

Prices drop

Between 1860 and 1890, more United States' land was turned into farmland than in the previous 253 years. When the weather was good, all this farmland created too much corn and wheat. Farmers had to keep cutting prices in order to sell their crops.

In 1881, a bushel of wheat sold for $1.19. In 1894, the price dropped to 49 cents. Many small farmers gave up. Others joined groups, such as the National Grange. This large group demanded that railroads lower their transportation prices. They found other ways to cut farming costs.

▲ After the land rush on September 16, 1893, these **homesteaders** lined up at the **land office** to record their **claims.** The land became the town of Perry, Oklahoma.

◀ People with small farms could walk through their fields and cut the grain by hand. But if farmers had large fields, it could take weeks of backbreaking work to harvest the crops. By the 1890s, steam engines provided power for the machines that turned the soil and harvested the grain. These workers are gathering cut wheat for the steam powered machines that separate out the grain. Sacks of grain are then loaded onto wagons. They will be stored in barns or transported by railroad to food factories in the East and South.

OIL!
Valuable oil lay under the ground in Oklahoma. The first successful oil well was drilled near Chelsea in 1889. In the next few years, several oil fields were discovered near Tulsa.

23

THE AMERICAN INDIANS

By 1893, almost all American Indian tribes lived on U.S. government reservations. Over the centuries, roads, train tracks, farms, and buildings replaced Indian land, villages, and hunting grounds. All these people had left was their beliefs, languages, and customs.

Life on the **reservations** often seemed hopeless. There were no animals to hunt. Crops did not grow well. By 1900, there were only 237,000 American Indians in the United States. How could the Indians survive? Some U.S. citizens insisted that Indian children were the answer. Children must be taught "not as Indians, but as Americans."

The Carlisle School
In 1879, a white man named Richard Pratt convinced tribes in Dakota **Territory** to send 82 children to a special school in Carlisle, Pennsylvania. When the children arrived, a barber cut their hair. Their moccasins were thrown away, and teachers gave uniforms to the boys and dresses to the girls. The children were never allowed to speak Indian languages or sing Indian songs. Teachers taught them reading, writing, and arithmetic. Boys learned to build and make things. Girls learned to cook and sew.

Within a few years, there were 1,000 students at the Carlisle School. Many similar schools opened across the country. Some American Indians thought these schools would help their children make a good life. Others hated the schools. They did not want children to forget their Indian customs.

▼ Indian children felt strange in their new clothes and shoes. Teachers were very strict as they taught the children useful skills to help them get jobs.

JIM THORPE
Jim Thorpe was an Olympic track-and-field champion in 1912 and a professional football and baseball player from 1910 to 1929. He was part Potawatomi and part Sac-Fox Indian. He was born near the town of Prague, Oklahoma, which was settled during the 1891 land rush. He attended the Carlisle School.

▼ Every student at the Carlisle School took music lessons. The school marching band was famous. Whenever a new U.S. president started his term, the Carlisle School band marched in the **inauguration** parade.

Government officials sent some children to the school without their parents' permission.

RIGHTS
In 1901, members of the **Five Civilized Tribes** were made United States citizens. In 1924, the Indian Citizenship Act granted citizenship to the rest of the tribes across the United States.

25

THE STATE OF OKLAHOMA

The state we now call Oklahoma went through many changes. First it was wide-open land along cattle trails and trading routes. In 1830, it became a homeland forced upon American Indians. By 1880, white settlers started to want it. In 1907, Oklahoma became the 46th state.

As in the rest of the nation, the towns of Oklahoma took on a modern look by 1900. By 1905, electric trolleys rolled through Guthrie and other towns. People worked in factories, mines, and farms, mostly earning a good living.

Before 1907, maps of the United States labeled Oklahoma as Twin Territories. The western part was called Oklahoma **Territory.** The eastern part was called Indian Territory and was the home of the Cherokee Nation, some other American Indian tribes, plus five times as many white people as American Indians. Many people in Indian Territory wanted it to become a separate state called Sequoyah. President Theodore Roosevelt would not allow this. In 1907 both territories, together, became the state of Oklahoma.

To celebrate, government officials held a pretend wedding between a cowboy and an American Indian woman. They wanted to show that Indian and white communities were blending together. This was not totally true. The American Indians had been told to change their ways, and many of them did. But the Indian **customs** and beliefs did not die. To this day, many American Indians follow the traditional ways of their tribes.

▲ For years, farmers turned too much grassy land into wheat fields. They did not know they were making it hard for the soil to hold rainwater. From 1935 to 1938, there was almost no rain in Oklahoma. The crops died and the fields turned to dust. Strong winds blew the dust everywhere. People called Oklahoma, Kansas, and southeastern Colorado the Dust Bowl.

▶ In 1907, Oklahoma City had brick buildings, high-fashion stores, hotels, and restaurants. In 1910, the state capitol was moved from Guthrie to Oklahoma City. The Lee-Huckins Hotel became a temporary capitol building. A permanent building was finished in 1917. The first parking meter in the world was invented and used in Oklahoma City in 1935.

LAND RIGHTS

In 1934, Congress passed the Indian Reorganization Act. It stopped the government from taking away **reservation** land from the American Indians. It gave back rights for some reservation land to American Indians.

RESERVATIONS

There are about 285 Indian reservations in the United States today. There are about 2.4 million American Indian and Alaskan natives (Inuits and Aleuts) in the nation. About half of them live on reservations.

Many people there earn a living by working on farms, making products, and running businesses and gambling casinos. Problems with education and health are common on reservations.

HISTORICAL MAP OF THE UNITED STATES

This map shows the United States in 1890. There were 44 states. Until 1889, North and South Dakota were called Dakota **Territory.** Once, American Indians lived throughout the continent. By 1890, the United States government forced them off their land and onto **reservations** throughout the **Great Plains** and the West. Before railroads reached Texas, cowboys used cattle trails from Texas to Kansas and Missouri. By the 1890s, five railroads stretched across the continent.

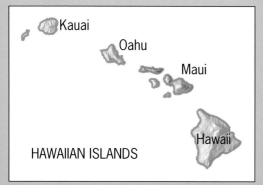

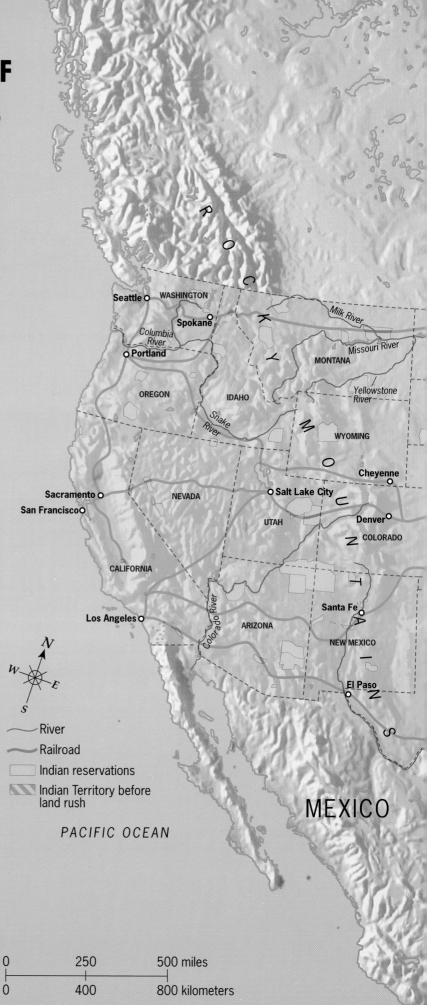

Hudson Bay

CANADA

MINNESOTA

NORTH DAKOTA

Lake Superior

SOUTH DAKOTA

WISCONSIN

Missouri River

Minneapolis

Mississippi River

IOWA

Milwaukee

Lake Michigan

MICHIGAN

Lake Huron

Detroit

Lake Ontario

NEW YORK

MAINE

VERMONT

NEW HAMPSHIRE

MASSACHUSETTS
Boston

RHODE ISLAND

CONNECTICUT

New York City

St. Lawrence

Chicago

Lake Erie

Cleveland

PENNSYLVANIA

Delaware River

Hudson River

NEW JERSEY

Philadelphia

NEBRASKA

ILLINOIS

INDIANA

OHIO

Pittsburgh

DELAWARE

MARYLAND

Washington, D.C.

ATLANTIC OCEAN

Independence

St. Louis

Ohio River

WEST VIRGINIA

VIRGINIA

KANSAS

Abilene

MISSOURI

KENTUCKY

James River

Dodge City

Mississippi River

TENNESSEE

NORTH CAROLINA

OKLAHOMA

Stillwater

Guthrie

Kingfisher

Oklahoma City

Norman

Arkansas River

Memphis

SOUTH CAROLINA

APPALACHIAN MOUNTAINS

Atlanta

Charleston

Birmingham

ARKANSAS

GEORGIA

Savannah

Dallas

MISSISSIPPI

ALABAMA

TEXAS

LOUISIANA

Jacksonville

New Orleans

FLORIDA

Houston

San Antonio

Rio Grande River

GULF OF MEXICO

29

CARIBBEAN SEA

GLOSSARY

boomer someone who wants to join a rush of settlers to a new area

border line that separates one country, state, or region from another

capital town or city where the government of a state or country is located. Government offices are located in the capitol building.

cattle drive long journey to walk cows, bulls, and other cattle from a ranch to a town where they are loaded onto trains

claim to say that an area of land belongs to you. The land is also called a claim.

Congress part of the United States government in which representatives make laws

custom special way of doing things

Five Civilized Tribes Cherokee, Chickasaw, Choctaw, Creek, and Seminole tribes who first lived in the Carolinas, Georgia, Alabama, Mississippi, Tennessee, and Florida. Thousands of them

were forced to move to Oklahoma. They were called "civilized tribes" because they had a written language and their lifestyle was similar in many ways to white settlers. These ways included raising crops and cattle, making laws, and building schools and churches.

Great Plains enormous area of grassland east of the Rocky Mountains. North to south, it stretches 2,500 miles (4,020 km) from Canada to Texas. Western Oklahoma is part of the Great Plains.

harvest gathering crops from a field after they have grown

homestead house and land around it. A person who owns a homestead is called a homesteader.

idleness doing nothing

immigrant someone who moves from another country

inauguration ceremony to put someone in office, such as the president of a country

land office place where new settlers sign papers to claim their land

locust type of grasshopper that swarms in groups of thousands and eats crops

nomadic wandering instead of living in one place

plow use a machine to cut up soil and turn it over before planting seeds. The machine is also called a plow.

reservation area of land set aside by the government for a special purpose, such as a place for American Indians to live

settler person who makes a home in a new place

slave person who is owned by another person and is usually forced to work for that person

sod piece of earth with grass and roots

sooner during the land rush, someone who arrived at the new land a few days before others were allowed in.

Today residents of Oklahoma are nicknamed Sooners.

surrender give up or admit you cannot win a battle

territory in the United States, an area of land that is not yet a state. Once a territory had 60,000 citizens, it could be admitted as a new state.

tipi cone-shaped tent made of animal skins

treaty written agreement, usually between two nations. The United States government made treaties with American Indian tribes, taking Indian land and giving land, food, and care elsewhere.

Unassigned Land land in Oklahoma that was not turned over to any American Indian tribe when the United States government gave them western land

TIMELINE OF EVENTS IN THIS BOOK

1828 United States government sets up Indian **Territory** as a place to move eastern tribes

1830 Congress passes the Indian Removal Act, forcing all American Indians to move west of the Mississippi River

1838 to 1839 One of the worst forced marches of American Indians to Indian Territory takes place, giving all such marches the name Trail of Tears

1862 Congress passes the Homestead Act to give western land to new **settlers**

1861 to 1865 Members of the **Five Civilized Tribes** fight for the South in the Civil War, fought between states in the South and states in the North

1876 Battle is fought at the Little Bighorn River in Montana, where the Sioux, Cheyenne, and Arapaho defeat Custer's soldiers

1877 Chief Joseph of the Nez Perce tribe **surrenders** and takes his people to Indian Territory

1879 The Carlisle School opens in Pennsylvania to educate American Indian children in the ways of the United States

1886 Apache chief, Geronimo, surrenders and moves his people to a **reservation**

1887 The Dawes Act takes away a tribe's right to own vast open land but it gives sections of land to each Indian tribe

1889 Oklahoma's first oil-producing well is drilled near Chelsea

1889 First Oklahoma land rush occurs as United States government opens **Unassigned Land** in Indian Territory to **homesteaders**

1890 Hundreds of American Indians are killed in the last battle between Indians and the Army, fought at Wounded Knee Creek, South Dakota.

1890 Congress passes the Oklahoma Organic Act, turning most of the western part of Indian Territory into Oklahoma Territory

1891 Land rush for land formerly given to Sac-Fox, Iowa, Shawnee, and Potawatomi Indians

1892 Land rush for land formerly given to Cheyenne and Arapaho

1893 Land rush for land in Cherokee Outlet, Tonkawa, and Pawnee reservations

1895 Land rush for land in Mexican Kickapoo reservation

1907 Oklahoma becomes the 46th state and Indian Territory ceases to exist

BOOKS TO READ
Durnett, Deanne. *Oklahoma.* Farmington Hills, Mich.: Gale Group, 2003.

Haines, J. D. *Wild and Woolly: Tales from Oklahoma Territorial Days.* Austin, Tex.: Eakin Press, 2003.

PLACES TO VISIT
Oklahoma Territorial Museum and Carnegie Library
406 E. Oklahoma
Guthrie, OK 73044-3317
Phone: (405) 282-1889

Fort Gibson Historic Site and Interpretive Center
907 N. Garrison
Fort Gibson, OK 74434
Telephone: (918) 478-4088

Humphrey Heritage Village
West Garriott and 4th
Enid, OK 73702
Telephone: (580) 237-1907

Cherokee Strip Museum
2617 Fir
Perry, OK 73077
Telephone: (580) 336-2405

INDEX

African Americans 9,
20
American Indians 3,
5–8, 10–12, 14,
18–20, 24–28, 30,
31
Apache 11
Arapaho 6, 7, 11, 19,
31
Arapahoe 20

bank 8, 18, 19
beef 12, 22
Boley 20
boomers 12, 14, 30
buffalo 7–9, 11

California 12
Carlisle School 24–25,
31
cattle 6, 12, 14, 22,
26, 30
Chelsea, OK 23
Cherokee 6, 7, 15,
16, 19, 26, 30
Cheyenne 11, 19, 31
Chickasaw 6, 15, 30
Chirichua 10
Choctaw 6
claim 14, 15, 20, 23,
30
clothes and clothing 6,
10, 21, 22, 24
Comanche 6, 7
Congress 6, 8, 12,
14, 18, 30, 31
Crazy Horse, Chief 10
Creek 6, 30
crops 6, 20, 22–24,
30
Custer, Lieutenant
George 11
customs 6, 24, 26, 30

Dakota 10, 11, 24,
28, 31

Dawes Act 12
disease 5, 11
dust 16, 18, 20, 26
Dust Bowl 26

factories 10, 12, 23,
26
farmers 6, 8, 12, 14,
20, 22, 23
farms 5, 22, 24, 26
Five Civilized Tribes 6,
7, 25, 30, 31
food 5, 6, 10, 20, 23,
30

Geronimo 10, 11, 31
Ghost Dance 11
gold 5, 12
Great Plains 6–10, 12,
28, 30
Guthrie, OK 17,
18–19, 26, 31

Henry, Hank 15, 16
homestead 8, 12, 14,
30, 31
homesteaders 8, 9,
12, 14, 18, 20, 22,
23
horse 4, 5, 15, 16
hotels 18, 19, 26
hunters and hunting 3,
6, 7, 9, 10, 14, 24

immigrants 5, 12, 30
Indian Citizenship Act
25
Indian Removal Act 6,
31
Indian Territory 3, 6, 7,
8, 12, 15, 18, 31
Indian Wars 10–11

Kansas 6, 12, 14, 20,
28
Kiowa 6, 7

land 5, 6, 8, 11, 12,
14, 15, 18, 21, 22,
26, 27, 30, 31
land office 15, 16, 23,
30
land rights 27
land rush 3–5, 16, 18,
19, 24, 31
Little Bighorn 11, 31
locusts 8, 30

Manifest Destiny 5
McCormick, Cyrus 22
Mississippi River 3, 6,
31
Missouri 28
Montana 11, 31

National Grange 23
Nevada 12
New Mexico 10
Nez Perce 11, 31

oil 23
Oklahoma 3–6, 10,
12, 14, 17–21, 23,
24, 26, 30
Oregon 15
Osage 6

Payne, David 12
plow 22, 30
Potawatomi 19, 24,
31
Pratt, Richard 24

railroad 9, 10, 12, 14,
20, 23, 28
ranches 10, 30
reservations 10, 11,
13, 14, 19, 24, 27,
28, 30, 31
Roosevelt, President
26

Sac-Fox 19, 24, 31

schools 6, 20, 24, 30
Seminole 6, 30
Sequoyah 26
settlers 3, 4, 6–8, 10,
12, 18, 20, 26, 30
Shoshone 13
silver 12
Sioux 10, 11
Sitting Bull 11
slaves 5, 9, 30
sod 8–9, 30
sooners 14, 30
steam engines 23
store 18, 19, 20–22,
26

tents 15, 16, 21
Texas 8, 12, 14, 28,
30
Thorpe, Jim 24
tipis 7, 30
towns 5, 8, 14, 17,
18, 26, 30
Trail of Tears 7, 31
treaties 6, 30
Twin Territories 26

Unassigned Land 12,
14, 19, 30, 31
United States (U.S.)
3–7, 10–12, 13, 15,
18, 25, 28, 30, 31

wagon 4, 15, 16, 18,
20, 22, 23
water 6, 8, 14, 17, 20
weather 8, 14, 22, 23
wheat 8, 12, 22, 23,
26
Wichita 6
Wounded Knee Creek
11, 31
Wyoming 10, 13